T0082215

unshakable
moxie

unshakable moxie

GROWING a RESILIENT FAITH

Lina AbuJamra

Our Daily Bread
Publishing.

Unshakable Moxie: Growing a Resilient Faith
© 2024 by Lina AbuJamra

All rights reserved.

Requests for permission to quote from this book should be directed to: Permissions Department, Our Daily Bread Publishing, PO Box 3566, Grand Rapids, MI 49501, or contact us by email at permissionsdept@odb.org.

Personal quotations excerpted from the *Unshakable Moxie* video series: Used by permission.

Scripture quotations, unless otherwise indicated, are taken from the ESV® Bible (The Holy Bible, English Standard Version®), copyright © 2001 by Crossway, a publishing ministry of Good News Publishers. Used by permission. All rights reserved.

Scripture quotations marked NIV are taken from the Holy Bible, New International Version®, NIV®. Copyright © 1973, 1978, 1984, 2011 by Biblica, Inc.™ Used by permission of Zondervan. All rights reserved worldwide. www.zondervan.com.

Scripture quotations marked NLT are taken from the Holy Bible, New Living Translation, copyright © 1996, 2004, 2015 by Tyndale House Foundation. Used by permission of Tyndale House Publishers, Inc., Carol Stream, Illinois 60188. All rights reserved.

Interior design by Michael J. Williams

Library of Congress Cataloging-in-Publication Data

Names: AbuJamra, Lina, author.
Title: Unshakable moxie : growing a resilient faith, a Bible study / Lina AbuJamra.
Description: Grand Rapids, MI : Our Daily Bread Ministries, [2024] | Summary: "This Bible study opens up the conversation on real life faith development. It helps women answer the questions: how do some women get unshakable moxie, or that resilient faith? How can the woman doing this study develop unshakable faith like that?"-- Provided by publisher.
Identifiers: LCCN 2023029133 (print) | LCCN 2023029134 (ebook) | ISBN 9781640702639 (trade paperback) | ISBN 9781640702714 (epub)
Subjects: LCSH: Christian women--Religious life. | Faith--Biblical teaching. | Christian life. | BISAC: RELIGION / Biblical Studies / General | RELIGION / Christian Living / Women's Interests
Classification: LCC BV4527 .A243 2024 (print) | LCC BV4527 (ebook) | DDC 248.8/43- -dc23/eng/20230722
LC record available at https://lccn.loc.gov/2023029133
LC ebook record available at https://lccn.loc.gov/2023029134

Printed in the United States of America
24 25 26 27 28 29 30 31 / 8 7 6 5 4 3 2 1

CONTENTS

INTRODUCTION

I was ten years old when I first heard the name Joni Eareckson Tada. I was living in war-torn Beirut, Lebanon, at that time, my hometown. It was peaceful enough on that Sunday night for our missionary pastor to show us a movie, and we all sat back and watched the story of a woman who I now believe is the very definition of *moxie*.

When the movie began and Joni, who was thirty at the time, shared her inspiring story of living victoriously through Christ despite her quadriplegia, I had no idea how deeply my life would be affected by her. I can assure you that as a ten-year-old, I had no grasp of what the Bible taught about courage and faith nor what God had planned for me for the rest of my life. But I did learn one thing while watching the movie: I wanted whatever it was that Joni had. I yearned, deep in my bones, for the strength I saw portrayed in those ninety minutes. I was moved to tears by her wrestling with God. I was riveted by Joni's focus and her ability to see God's goodness even in the face of tragedy.

To say that my life was changed by Joni on that night is an understatement. Even without having the language for what was happening to me back in the '80s, I knew that my life needed to follow a different path. I wanted the Jesus way.

Joni's story changed my life. And that's the thing about the stories we hear—they capture our hearts in a way nothing else can. Stories elevate our vision. They fill us with dreams for more. They ignite hope in our hearts, assuring us that because someone else was able to overcome great trials, we might be able to do the same.

It's why I think Jesus so often used stories in relating to people. And it's one of the main reasons why the Scriptures capture our attention. We connect with stories about struggle and faith. We celebrate when the underdog rises to the challenge and the weak rise from the ashes. We rejoice when battles that seem doomed to fail are eventually won. We explode with hope that the hero in the story of our own lives will soon find us and rescue us from our deepest failures and worst nightmares.

When it comes to God's Word, Jesus is and has always been our hero. As we'll see in the coming weeks, he's the reason Joni's life was transformed from hopelessness to joy. He is the one who freed Ruth Chou Simons from the burden of striving and gifted her a life of grace. He was the one who released Bernice King from the chains of unforgiveness to the freedom of love. He is the one who helped Katie Lewis realize the value of dark times. And Jesus is the one who taught me that failure is not final and that the resilience of faith is made stronger through the fire of suffering.

In a culture where we're taught that strength is boiled down to our ability to pull ourselves up by our bootstraps and fight our way out of any predicament, the kind of moxie—resilient faith—that Jesus offers is indeed radical. It's mind-boggling. It's divine. The deeper our culture drifts into the post-Christian era we're already living in, the more radical the way of Jesus proves to be.

To develop the type of unshakable moxie presented in the lives of the women in this video series, we will need to root ourselves in the Word of God like never before. We will need to surround ourselves with a great cloud of witnesses and run with endurance the race that is set before us. As we look to Jesus, the author and finisher of our faith, and resolve to endure like never before, there is a joy coming that is beyond anything we have ever experienced or imagined. It's how we develop unshakable moxie. It's how we live triumphantly in the face of trouble.

How to Use This Study

In this Bible study, we will explore what characteristics produce resolute faith. We will focus on knowing Christ changes us, overcoming hardship, redeeming failure, growing out of disillusionment, experiencing and practicing forgiveness, and living by grace.

Unshakable Moxie provides a variety of ways to explore the Bible and the theme of resolute faith. Here is the suggested path to work through each session:

First, take a few minutes to read and work through the first couple of pages of the session, up to the QR code. If you want to use the same Bible translation that is printed in the study, that is the English Standard Version, but you can use whichever version is most helpful to you.

Next, scan the QR code and watch the video for the session. Journal thoughts and questions as you watch. We've followed this with some specific questions to promote contemplation of the video message. The videos feature Moriah Smallbone and Toni Collier talking with five other women of moxie. The first video introduces you to Moriah and Toni.

The Bible Study section can be broken up into several smaller sessions depending on your time. Some questions will be answered quickly while others are more thought provoking. These can be answered in groups or during individual study time. And it's okay if you don't have time to complete each section of the study. You can return to any section as time allows.

The Lectio Divina section invites you to read a Scripture passage three different times, whether in a group or as an individual activity. Try it with each chapter to experience how Scripture can speak to us.

We end each session with quotable messages. Consider sharing these on social media to encourage others to grow their own resilient faith.

No matter where you find yourself in your faith journey, my prayer is that this study will challenge you to follow the example of Jesus even as you learn from the stories of those featured.

When all is said and done, the Christian life can truly be summed up in one word: trust. Whether you've had years of practice trusting Jesus with your life or you've just started following our Savior, the invitation in this guide is for you to accept the offer that Jesus once extended to the worn-out crowd around Him when He urged them to come and find rest in Him.

So whether it's the story of Joni that unleashes your longing for more of God in your life, like it did for me, or another one of the awesome stories of women with moxie, or the stories of men and women in the Bible, may you continue to grow in resolute faith as you become even more grounded in God's Word and more focused on the person of Jesus, to whom be all honor and glory forever.

I'm so honored we're on this journey together. And if by some offbeat chance you've resonated with my story of moxie, I hope you trust me enough to believe me when I tell you that there's nothing more you need in your life than Jesus. Find Him in His Word. Experience Him through the Spirit in every detail of your life. Then let Him unleash your life for His glory forever.

This is the life of moxie.

Your friend,
Lina

* If you are leading a small group study, you can download a leader's guide. Visit https://read.odb.org/unshakable-moxie/.

Session 1

THE JOURNEY BEGINS: DISCOVERING MOXIE

Moxie[1]
mox·ie /ˈmäk-sē/ noun

1: ENERGY, PEP
   woke up full of *moxie*
2: COURAGE, DETERMINATION
   "it takes . . . *moxie* to pull up roots and go to a land where the culture and probably the language are totally foreign." –M. J. McClary
3: KNOW-HOW
   was impressed with his musical *moxie* and hired him as a soloist

This Week's Bible Study Goals

- Understand who God is as a trustworthy, loving Savior
- Believe who you are in Christ and explore how faith shapes and changes your life

Your Personal Goals for the Week

- Become comfortable sharing authentically and transparently with one another
- Begin to build trust within your group
- Ponder and talk about areas you wish to grow in
- Add any other goals you may have_____

_____

Memory Verse

But now thus says the LORD, he who created you, O Jacob, he who formed you, O Israel: "Fear not, for I have redeemed you; I have called you by name, you are mine."

Isaiah 43:1

Get Started

Share about a time when you struggled with knowing who you are or a time when you struggled to know your purpose. What did you wrestle with?

_____

_____

_____

_____

_____

Who or what comes to mind when you think about a woman with moxie?

_____

_____

_____

_____

_____

Meet Moriah Smallbone and Toni Collier

While watching the video, record any observations, memorable moments, personal connections, or questions you have.

Video Discussion Questions

What part of Moriah and Toni's story did you connect with the most? Why?

Moriah mentioned a word she picks for the year on her birthday. If you had to choose a word to describe your year so far, what would it be?

What circumstances from your past have caused you to question your identity like Moriah and Toni have?

Moriah mentioned that prayer can be "awkward." How would you describe your prayer life in one word?

Toni talked about how her past trauma has affected her view of God. How have your past hurts affected how you relate to God?

Toni and Moriah are authentic and transparent by the end of the film. They share their apprehensions and hopes for the upcoming weeks. What apprehensions do you have as we start on this journey? What are you hopeful for?

_____

_____

_____

Bible Study

Complete this session during the week to discuss with your small group.

What does it mean to have *moxie*? Where do grit, courage, and perseverance come from?

We're going to spend the next six weeks together listening to the stories of women who exemplify moxie. We are going to learn their secrets to true strength. Though the stories will vary in their details, one theme will remain the same: real strength is born out of weakness.

Interestingly, we're living in a culture that champions women like never before. Today's woman is encouraged to be strong and to own her power. Our present-day culture looks up to women who are fiercely independent and able to hold their own against any challenges thrown their way. The post-feminist movement has opened doors to women like never before: women don't just vote but are able to hold the highest office as well. Most women not only have the right to have as many children as they want but women can now also choose not to have children and not be scorned by their decision. Women can participate in the workforce in any capacity and are expected to fight for themselves and the people they love.

While many of the changes we've seen in our culture have opened the doors for women to live out their full potential and calling, it's important for us to stop and think about what true strength really means, biblically speaking.

What is moxie when it comes to God's Word? What does a Jesus-following, God-fearing strong woman look like? Too many of us have taken cues from our culture instead of God's Word. As we embark on this journey together, my challenge to you is to stop long enough to give the Spirit of God a chance to show you what real courage looks like. My prayer for you is that you begin to see that God doesn't wait on cultural change to fulfill His calling in your life. As a follower of Jesus, you have been given the strength and the power to live courageously and to persevere to the end. But often, the strength that God looks for is not the same as the strength that we value in our culture.

What comes to mind when you think of the word *moxie*?

_____

_____

Describe what a strong woman looks like based on what you've been taught and observed in your life so far.

_____

_____

_____

When it comes to the idea of strength and courage, do you feel like you've been more influenced by culture or by God's Word? Share why you think this is the case.

_____

_____

_____

_____

Read John 4:1–30

Now when Jesus learned that the Pharisees had heard that Jesus was making and baptizing more disciples than John (although Jesus himself did not baptize, but only his disciples), he left Judea and departed again for Galilee. And he had to pass through Samaria. So he came to a town of Samaria called Sychar, near the field that Jacob had given to his son Joseph. Jacob's well was there; so Jesus, wearied as he was from his journey, was sitting beside the well. It was about the sixth hour.

A woman from Samaria came to draw water. Jesus said to her, "Give me a drink." (For his disciples had gone away into the city to buy food.) The Samaritan woman said to him, "How is it that you, a Jew, ask for a drink from me, a woman of Samaria?" (For Jews have no dealings with Samaritans.) Jesus answered her, "If you knew the gift of God, and who it is that is saying to you, 'Give me a drink,' you would have asked him, and he would have given you living water." The woman said to him, "Sir, you have nothing to draw water with, and the well is deep. Where do you get that living water? Are you greater than our father Jacob? He gave us the well and drank from it himself, as did his sons and his livestock." Jesus said to her, "Everyone who drinks of this water will be thirsty again, but whoever drinks of the water that I will give him will never be thirsty again. The water that I will give him will become in him a spring of water welling up to eternal life." The woman said to him, "Sir, give me this water, so that I will not be thirsty or have to come here to draw water."

Jesus said to her, "Go, call your husband, and come here." The woman answered him, "I have no husband." Jesus said to her, "You are right in saying, 'I have no husband'; for you have had five husbands, and the one you now have is not your husband. What you have said is true." The woman said to him, "Sir, I perceive that you are a prophet. Our fathers worshiped on this mountain, but you say that in Jerusalem is the place where people ought to worship." Jesus said to her, "Woman, believe me, the hour is coming when neither on this mountain nor in Jerusalem will you worship the Father. You worship what you do not know; we worship what we know, for salvation is from the Jews. But the hour is coming, and is now here, when the true worshipers will worship the Father in spirit and truth, for the Father is seeking such people to worship him. God is spirit, and those who worship him must worship in spirit and truth." The woman said to him, "I know that Messiah is coming (he who is called Christ). When he comes, he will tell us all things." Jesus said to her, "I who speak to you am he."

Just then his disciples came back. They marveled that he was talking with a woman, but no one said, "What do you seek?" or, "Why are you talking with her?" So the woman left her water jar and went away into town and said to the people, "Come, see a man who told me all that I ever did. Can this be the Christ?" They went out of the town and were coming to him.

Questions to Ponder

Describe the woman in this story in as much detail as possible. What are some of the facts we learn about her? What are some of the more subtle observations you might glean about her?

_____

_____

_____

Would you describe the Samaritan woman as a strong woman? Why or why not?

_____

_____

_____

What most surprises you about the way Jesus interacted with this woman?

_____

_____

_____

What is the main message that Jesus shared with the woman about who He is?

_____

_____

_____

By the time we get to verse 29, where she says to the people in her town: "Come, see a man who told me all that I ever did. Can this be the Christ?" the woman seems to have made a complete turn-around. What do you think happened to the woman through her encounter with Jesus?

It's interesting that the very woman who had tried so hard to avoid the crowd by going to the well at the hottest hour of the day (around noon) is the very woman who courageously ran back to the village to recruit the crowd to come and meet Jesus. It took courage, or dare I say, moxie, for the Samaritan woman to face her harshest critics with the good news about Jesus. It took the woman being set free from her own fears and insecurities to be able to own her past mistakes and step into her God-given future.

Put yourself in the Samaritan woman's shoes for a moment.

What is it about your past that you long to keep hidden?

_____

_____

_____

How does the idea that God already knows everything about you make you feel?

_____

_____

_____

It's easy to feel suffocated by the guilt of our past mistakes. It seems easier to choose to hide our worst mistakes than to admit them. Yet true freedom does not come from ignoring our worst selves; freedom comes from facing our worst issues and understanding that we are fully known and fully loved by God!

Read Romans 5:8. What do you learn about God's love for you?

_____

_____

Read Ephesians 2:8–10. What amount of work does God expect of you to earn your standing with Him?

Read Titus 3:5. Why does God choose to save us?

Read 2 Corinthians 5:17. What promise are we given the moment we receive Christ's gift of salvation? If you have received the gift, how have you seen that you are a "new creation" in your life?

Read 1 Peter 2:9–10. Describe the kind of person you have become in Christ Jesus.

Read Romans 8:1. Why do you think so many Christians still struggle with a deep sense of condemnation and guilt?

Read 1 John 3:1. This verse best explains the relationship God promises those who receive Him. How in your life have *you* experienced God's love? Be as specific as possible.

If you've never experienced God's love personally, you might be wondering how this happens. The Bible tells us that everyone who calls upon the name of the Lord will be saved (Romans 10:13). That includes you! Perhaps you need it spelled out even more clearly.

Read John 3:16–17. These verses are some of the most famous in the Bible. What is the basis of a relationship with Christ according to these verses?

_____

_____

_____

_____

Read John 1:11–12. Again we're told that salvation boils down to one thing: faith in Christ alone. Have you been granted the right to be called a child of God yet? Have you put your faith in Jesus? Do you believe in Jesus and in His death and resurrection? If not, what questions do you have? Consider talking about these questions with a Christian leader.

_____

_____

_____

_____

The Samaritan woman is fascinating. Here was a woman who didn't want to show her face to the rest of the villagers during normal hours of gathering water at the well. Yet by the time the story ends, the entire village has rallied to hear what she has to say about Christ, the Messiah (Savior). They even went to meet Christ for themselves (John 4:30). Because of this woman's words, many Samaritans met Jesus and believed in Him. This occurred all because a woman with a past met Jesus at the well at the hottest hour of the day. It's amazing how radical God's love is and how deeply it turns our whole lives upside down!

Read John 4:39–42. Describe what happened in the village due to the testimony of the Samaritan woman. What do you think caused this change in the hearts of the people?

_____

_____

_____

Jesus changes everything. The things that used to scare us no longer have power over us in Christ. The people who used to control us no longer hold power over us in Christ. The shame we held on to for so long has no place in our lives anymore in Christ. The future we envisioned is radically transformed by the love and power of Christ. The condemnation we've been so used to carrying loses its grip on us in Christ. Indeed, Jesus changes everything.

In what ways has your life been changed by Jesus?

_____

_____

Read Ephesians 2:8–10 again. Though we discussed it earlier, this time focus on verse 10. Has it ever occurred to you that you have been given a purpose for your life? Take some time and think about what your God-given purpose could be. Ask the Lord to reveal His purposes to you.

_____

_____

Application Questions

How is God equipping you to trust Him and receive His grace? Choose one or more of the questions below to answer in the space provided.

- Do you see yourself as a beloved child of God? What are the implications of this for your daily living?

- Do you have the courage to face your life and your past because you've been set free by the love of Jesus? What are some practical ways you can live your life like the Samaritan woman did?
- Identify two or three areas of your spiritual life that you struggle with.
- Dream about how you would like to grow in these areas. If you could be the healthiest version of yourself, what would that look like?

Lectio Divina

Our goal in this section is to experience the practice of quiet Scripture meditation in order to draw us closer to Jesus as a community. After each reading, answer the questions below, keeping your answers succinct and specific. Invite yourself to listen to God through His Word, allowing the Holy Spirit to move in you. Don't be afraid to share yourself authentically with others.

1 John 3:1–3 NIV

> See what great love the Father has lavished on us, that we should be called children of God! And that is what we are! The reason the world does not know us is that it did not know him. Dear friends, now we are children of God, and what we will be has not yet been made known. But we know that when Christ appears, we shall be like him, for we shall see him as he is. All who have this hope in him purify themselves, just as he is pure.

First Reading

What is one word or phrase that the Holy Spirit impresses on you?

_____

Second Reading

What do you feel? What specific situation in your life today relates to the passage?

_____

_____

_____

Third Reading

What is Christ's personal invitation to you from the Scripture?

_____

_____

Wrapping It Up

Consider sharing these quotes with your friends on social media.

*God, let me want you more than any
vision that you've given me.*
—Moriah Smallbone

● ● ●

*Nowhere does Jesus promise that you can
get all your dreams . . . if you follow Him.*
—Moriah Smallbone

● ● ●

*Jesus came to make things whole. You
don't have to worry about the future.*
—Toni Collier

● ● ●

*Real grit, real moxie, is being able to say,
"Right now, I'm not strong enough."*
—Toni Collier

● ● ●

*I don't want to run so hard that I
miss what real peace looks like.*
—Toni Collier

● ● ●

Session 2

FINDING THE BEAUTY IN GRACE

Grace[2]
/grās/ noun (from Latin *gratia*, favor, charm, thanks)

1 a: unmerited divine assistance given to humans for their regeneration or sanctification
  b: a virtue coming from God
  c: a state of sanctification enjoyed through divine assistance
2 a: approval, favor (e.g., stayed in his good *graces*)
  b: archaic: mercy, pardon
  c: a special favor: privilege (e.g., "each in his place, by right, not *grace*, shall rule his heritage" —Rudyard Kipling)
  d: disposition to or an act or instance of kindness, courtesy, or clemency
  e: a temporary exemption: reprieve

This Week's Bible Study Goals

- Understand God's never-ending extravagant grace in your life
- Practice a God-honoring response to God's grace

Your Personal Goals for the Week

- Recognize patterns in your life of trying to earn God's favor
- Continue to build trust within your group
- Prayerfully ask the Holy Spirit to speak clearly to you in areas you need to grow in
- Add any other goals you may have_____

_____

Memory Verse

*But he said to me, "My grace is sufficient for you, for
my power is made perfect in weakness." Therefore
I will boast all the more gladly of my weaknesses,
so that the power of Christ may rest upon me.*

2 Corinthians 12:9

Get Started

Think of a time that you were overwhelmed by a task or job that was too
much to handle. What did you do?

_____

_____

_____

_____

Describe yourself in a few words. Are you more of an achiever and a doer,
or do you tend to be easy going and let things go?

_____

_____

_____

_____

When you think about grace and truth, to which do you naturally gravi-
tate more?

_____

_____

_____

Meet Ruth Chou Simons

While watching the video, record any observations, memorable moments, personal connections, or questions you have.

Video Discussion Questions

What part of Ruth's story did you connect with the most?

_____

_____

_____

What are some of the ways you try to secure your worth through your own efforts?

_____

_____

_____

Ruth mentioned the story of Eve in Genesis 3. Despite having everything, Eve still was not content and strove for the one thing she thought would make her happiness complete. Is there anything in your life right now that you think would make you happy if you could just get a hold of it? What does the example of Eve teach you about your longings?

_____

_____

_____

Tell about a time you strove for something and attained it but found that it didn't fulfill you.

_____

_____

_____

Bible Study

Complete this session during the week to discuss with your small group.

Grace is one of the most overused words in the English language, and possibly one of the most misunderstood. We talk about *saying grace* before a meal, or we ask our teachers for a *grace period* when we've missed the deadline on a project. We expect the people we like to *grace* us with their presence. We point to a dancer and comment on her *grace*.

Yet grace is so much more than a posture. Grace is a gift God gives every single human being on a daily basis. When you come to think about it, grace is the reason our planet still exists.

If you've grown up around church people, then you may have come across some common definitions of grace: God's riches at Christ's expense, or unmerited favor of God. Both of these definitions are true, yet grace is so much more than that. I really like how Dallas Willard defines grace. He says that grace is God acting in my life to bring about what I cannot do on my own.[3] (Which happens to be pretty much everything!)

While the idea of grace sounds great to most of us (I mean, who doesn't want God to do everything on our behalf), the reality is that most of us sort of think we can do everything on our own. As Ruth described in the video, we live in a culture of striving and hustle that thinks along these lines: "Why settle for a B when you can get an A?" Like Ruth, you might have picked up the habit of striving to impress from a family who valued achievement over relationship. You might be tempted to carry that same mindset into your walk with the Lord. Many of us try to impress God with our abilities. We figure if we try hard enough, God will see how serious we are about Him. But it's only when we get to the end of our rope—after trying in vain to do everything a certain way—that we finally bother to look up. Yet looking up is precisely the point of following Jesus.

In the first session we spent some time talking about salvation and grace. The meetup between Christ and the Samaritan woman taught us that God loves us despite our struggles with sin. He is committed to us even though He already knows we're sinners. And while most Christians have come to terms with the notion of salvation by grace, the tension we face is in living our day-to-day Christian life by grace. We are much more fixated with trying to impress people—or even God—in our daily living, thinking that if we try hard enough, we might be accepted by others or eventually earn God's favor. So we try and try and try harder until we're finally worn out, exhausted, and spent. It's usually at this point in our lives that we finally give up. It's at this point that we finally cry out for help. And it's at this point that we're finally ready to see and receive this grace that God so lovingly grants us.

In your own experience or by observing others, what do you feel leads to exhaustion in the Christian life?

_____

_____

_____

_____

Why do you think we're so tempted to try to earn favor from others or even God?

_____

_____

_____

_____

It's easy to understand that our relationships with our earthly fathers affect the way we relate to our heavenly Father. For some, embracing the the idea of God as a father might even be a catalyst to reactivate feelings of deep trauma depending on your own relationship, or lack of one with your earthly fathers. The last thing you might imagine is turning to your Father God for grace. Just like Ruth, your whole understanding of fatherhood is marred by a watershed event that has impacted your ability to walk in freedom. Perhaps a better way to understand our heavenly Father is to let Jesus explain. In the parable of the prodigal, Jesus shows us the nuance between being saved by grace and living by grace in a story about two brothers and their grace-filled father. The father, as you might already know, is the very picture of what our heavenly Father is like. No matter what your family background is, this is a Father you're going to want to run toward, not away from. No matter what your past has held, the story of the prodigal is going to draw you closer to the heart of your heavenly Father.

Read Luke 15:11–32

And he said, "There was a man who had two sons. And the younger of them said to his father, 'Father, give me the share of property that is coming to me.' And he divided his property between them. Not many days later, the younger son gathered all he had and took a journey into a far country, and there he squandered his property in reckless living. And when he had spent everything, a severe famine arose in that country, and he began to be in need. So he went and hired himself out to one of the citizens of that country, who sent him into his fields to feed pigs. And he was longing to be fed with the pods that the pigs ate, and no one gave him anything.

"But when he came to himself, he said, 'How many of my father's hired servants have more than enough bread, but I perish here with hunger! I will arise and go to my father, and I will say to him, "Father, I have sinned against heaven and before you. I am no longer worthy to be called your son. Treat me as one of your hired servants."' And he arose and came to his father. But while he was still a long way off, his father saw him and felt compassion, and ran and embraced him and kissed him. And the son said to him, 'Father, I have sinned against heaven and before you. I am no longer worthy to be called your son.' But the father said to his servants, 'Bring quickly the best robe, and put it on him, and put a ring on his hand, and shoes on his feet. And bring the fattened calf and kill it, and let us eat and celebrate. For this my son was dead, and is alive again; he was lost, and is found.' And they began to celebrate.

"Now his older son was in the field, and as he came and drew near to the house, he heard music and dancing. And he called one of the servants and asked what these things meant. And he said to him, 'Your brother has come, and your father has killed the fattened calf, because he has received him back safe and sound.' But he was angry and refused to go in. His father came out and entreated him, but he answered his father, 'Look, these many years I have served you, and I never disobeyed your command, yet you never gave me a young goat, that I might celebrate with my friends. But when this son of yours came, who has devoured your property with prostitutes, you killed the fattened calf for him!' And he said to him, 'Son, you are always with me, and all that is mine is yours. It was fitting to celebrate and be glad, for this your brother was dead, and is alive; he was lost, and is found.'"

Questions to Ponder

The father in this story represents God the Father. Based on the parable, what are the character traits of the prodigal's father?

_____

_____

_____

Which of the two sons do you relate to the most and why?

_____

_____

_____

Focus on the younger brother first. What sort of welcome did he expect upon returning home? What sort of welcome did he deserve?

_____

_____

_____

What surprises you the most about the response of the father to the prodigal?

_____

_____

_____

_____

Have you ever experienced the kind of unconditional love that is portrayed in the story? If so, share how it made you feel.

_____

_____

_____

Now let's turn our focus to the older brother. Why was he angry?

_____

_____

_____

Does the response of the older brother surprise you or do you find yourself sympathetic to him?

_____

_____

_____

How did the father handle the older brother? Does his response surprise you? Why or why not?

_____

_____

_____

Which of the two sons do you think understood the concept of grace more? Why do you think that is?

_____

_____

_____

The picture of the younger son coming home and receiving His father's love and acceptance feels a little bit like a picture of God's grace to sinners at the moment of salvation. We're all sinners, choosing our own way in life, until we come to a place where we realize our desperate need for salvation. The moment we recognize the need for salvation, we have a choice to make: we can continue to live in our pigsty, or we can turn to our Father's home. God's grace is visible to us the moment we realize that our Father has been waiting for us all along with arms wide open.

It's a feel-good story. It's an awesome reality.

Was there ever a time in your life when you turned from your sin and ran into the arms of the Father? If yes, describe it. If no, write about why you haven't.

_____

_____

_____

_____

_____

The problem for most Christians is that we're a lot more like the older brother than we care to admit. Despite the fact that we've received salvation by grace in Christ alone, somewhere along the way we pick up the notion that we're supposed to earn God's favor. We lose sight of all the goodness given to us by our Father. We forget all the blessings we're afforded in Christ. Instead of feeling joy in our Christian walk, we trudge around discouraged and exhausted until eventually the truth comes out: we're mad about our lives. Just like the older brother in the parable, we feel we've been short-changed. We've done our part, but God hasn't done His. We expected it to be easier; we hoped for more reward in exchange for our hard work.

Despite having been saved by grace, some of us seem to spend the majority of our Christian life living a graceless existence.

But there is good news: God's grace never ends or runs out. It's ours when we need it. It might take an utter failure or devastating disappointment to get us to the point of acknowledging the need for it. However, God's grace ensures that when we're at our lowest, His grace is ours for the taking.

Let's explore this concept of grace even more.

Read Galatians 2:20. If you were to explain the Christian life to someone based on this verse, what would you say?

———————————————————————————

———————————————————————————

In what practical ways can you apply Galatians 2:20 in your life?

———————————————————————————

———————————————————————————

Read Galatians 5:16–25. What does it look like to live by the flesh versus living by the Spirit?

———————————————————————————

———————————————————————————

Read Romans 5:20. Describe God's solution for those who struggle with persistent sin in their lives.

———————————————————————————

———————————————————————————

It's impossible to live the Christian life by our own efforts. It's doomed to fail. Jesus himself told us that apart from Him we can do nothing (John 15:5).

As for the parable, the older brother could have given up struggling to work hard for his father and trying to impress his father; the older brother should have understood that all the father wanted was for his son to enjoy the gift of *being* with his father. The father lovingly reminded his older son of this bedrock truth: "Son, you are always with me, and all that is mine is yours." Jesus called this state of being with God the Father "abiding."

Read John 15:5–9. What does the concept of abiding mean?

_____

_____

Is there an older Christian in your life who comes to mind when you think about abiding in Christ? What are some practical things about them that cause you to think of the concept of abiding?

_____

_____

The truth is that most of us don't understand what it means to abide until we need to abide. It's usually the trials of life that bring us to a place of desperate need for the Savior. It's usually in moments of crisis that we finally turn to God and find that He's been waiting for us all along. C. S. Lewis summarized it best when he wrote: "God whispers to us in our pleasures, speaks in our conscience, but shouts in our pain. Pain is God's megaphone to rouse a deaf world."[4]

Here's how the apostle Paul explains abiding in Christ.

Read 2 Corinthians 12:7–10.
What was Paul's thorn in the flesh? Why do you think the Bible describes it as it does?

_____

_____

How do you define God's grace based on these verses?

_____

_____

_____

_____

Does it bring you comfort or frustrate you to hear God's solution to Paul's problem? Explain.

_____

_____

When it comes to unshakable moxie, how do these verses refine the definition of moxie for you?

_____

_____

It's only when grace is truly received that worship is genuinely given. It's the person who has been the recipient of God's massive and unending grace that is able to radically give his or her all back to God. Do you ever wonder what the next chapter was for the prodigal son? Do you wonder how he spent the rest of his life? Do you ever think about whether the older brother finally understood the meaning of grace? Did he remain stuck in his bitterness and resentment or did his father's love change him?

God's Word gives us a few examples of lives that were radically changed by grace.

Read Luke 7:36–47.
Why did the woman pour ointment from the alabaster flask onto Jesus's feet?

_____

_____

What was Jesus's response to the woman's act of worship?

_____

_____

What was Simon's response to the woman's offering? Why did he respond that way?

_____

_____

The only response to God's unrelenting grace in our lives is radical abandon. The sinful woman understood that no sacrifice was too great, no act too humble for her Savior who had lovingly forgiven her everything. Though her act of worship shocked those who were watching, and may have brought them some discomfort, her heart was evident to her Savior. "Her sins, which are many, are forgiven—for she loved much." This was true worship!

Application Questions

How is God equipping you to trust Him and receive His grace? Choose one or more of the questions below to answer in the space provided.

- Are you living the exhausted Christian life or are you depending on God's grace in your life?
- Have you received God's grace for something in your life that you regretted? How did this gift of grace impact your life?
- Have you ever been given a second chance at a mistake you made in your life? Tell about that experience.
- Recount ways that God has used "thorns" (trials, opposition, weaknesses) in your life to show His faithfulness or strength to bring about something good in your life.
- If your life were over and you were to meet Jesus today, is there anything in your life that you wish you could do differently? How might you start changing right now?

_____

_____

_____

_____

Lectio Divina

Our goal in this section is to experience the practice of quiet Scripture meditation in order to draw us closer to Jesus as a community. After each reading, answer the questions below, keeping your answers succinct and specific. Invite yourself to listen to God through His Word allowing the Holy Spirit to move in you. Don't be afraid to share yourself authentically with others.

2 Corinthians 12:8–10 NLT

> Three different times I begged the Lord to take it away. Each time he said, "My grace is all you need. My power works best in weakness." So now I am glad to boast about my weaknesses, so that the power of Christ can work through me. That's why I take pleasure in my weaknesses, and in the insults, hardships, persecutions, and troubles that I suffer for Christ. For when I am weak, then I am strong.

First Reading

What is one word or phrase that the Holy Spirit impresses on you?

_____

Second Reading

What do you feel? What specific situation in your life today relates to the passage?

_____

_____

_____

Third Reading

What is Christ's personal invitation to you from the Scripture?

_____

_____

Wrapping It Up

Consider sharing these quotes with your friends on social media.

You don't have to be blooming to be growing.
—Ruth Chou Simons

● ● ●

God is much more interested in you finding
Him than in you finding a solution.
—Ruth Chou Simons

● ● ●

Instead of looking for a way out,
start looking for a Way Maker.
—Toni Collier

● ● ●

God wants your heart more than
He wants anything else.
—Ruth Chou Simons

● ● ●

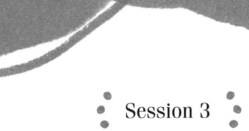

Session 3

UNCOVERING RESILIENT FAITH

Resilient[5]
re·sil·ient /ri-ˈzil-yənt/ adjective

characterized or marked by resilience: such as
- a: capable of withstanding shock without permanent deformation or rupture
- b: tending to recover from or adjust easily to misfortune or change

This Week's Bible Study Goals

- Understand how God uses your suffering to make you stronger
- Learn to see the painful places in your life as the very means for your growth

Your Personal Goals for the Week

- Honestly assess what's at the heart of your struggle and expectations in the Christian life
- Ponder and talk about areas you wish to grow in
- Continue to build trust within your group by praying for one another
- Add any other goals you may have

Memory Verse

*Count it all joy, my brothers [and sisters], when
you meet trials of various kinds, for you know that
the testing of your faith produces steadfastness.*

James 1:2–3

Get Started

Think about the one or two most painful trials you've ever had to live through. How did they affect your relationship with God?

_____

_____

_____

_____

What are some of the expectations you had when you started your walk with Jesus?

_____

_____

_____

_____

What is your first reaction when you hear someone tell you that your struggle will make you stronger?

_____

_____

_____

Meet Lina AbuJamra

While watching the video, record any observations, memorable moments, personal connections, or questions you have.

Video Discussion Questions

What stood out to you from the video?

What are some of the ways you identified with the struggle to trust God?

Have you ever experienced the pain of being disappointed and wounded by the church? If so and if you are comfortable, share more about that experience.

What is your response to someone who has experienced deep disappointment in the church?

How did it change your view of the struggle when you heard about the ways God has used Lina's pain to lead to her work with refugees?

Bible Study

Complete this session during the week to discuss with your small group.

It's not a matter of *if* you'll ever have a crisis of faith but *when* you'll have a crisis of faith. Anyone who has walked with Jesus for any length of time will learn this soon enough. While at first glance this idea sounds like a warning, the truth is that wrestling with God is not always a bad thing. Our struggle with God is what God often uses to bring us to our knees and allows us to trust Him even more deeply.

Men and women throughout Scripture struggled to believe God. The very people we consider the fathers of our faith weren't always the heroes of faith we think of today. They were actually a lot more like us—flesh and bones with desires and longings that often seemed to be the very things God was holding back from them. You can go all the way back to Genesis and see examples of this. Think about Abraham's longing for an heir, Joseph's dream to fulfill God's call on his life, Moses's desire to deliver his people, David's hope to build a house for God, and the Old Testament prophets' prayers to see the salvation of Israel. Over and over again we read accounts of people who wondered how God could promise something and then hold back from delivering that very thing that He so lovingly promised. The New Testament is no different. Whether it's Peter's desire to stand up for Jesus, or Paul's prayer to see his people turn back to Jesus, or John the beloved's wondering how he could be exiled to Patmos when the world needed to hear about Jesus, the same battle for faith rages. Is God really as good as He promises to be? Is God good enough to be trusted completely, even when life isn't going exactly as we hoped it would?

Your life and mine are not so different. We step into our relationship with Jesus hoping, believing, trusting that God will do everything He promises. It doesn't take long for that hope to turn into disappointment. The God-given desires of our hearts become a mirage in our rearview mirror, and the delays in our lives threaten to choke us. Our questions deepen while our joy shrinks. Why doesn't God seem to care about our pain? Where is God when we need Him the most? What is God up to in our lives during the times when it feels like we're walking through an unending desert alone?

This week's study will focus on these questions. We're going to try to understand what's at the heart of our struggles. We're going to ask God to search us and to know us and to help us see the light at the end of the dark tunnel we're in. I pray that we come out of this week stronger and more rooted in the truth of who God is—a faithful God who always keeps His promises.

If you've ever wondered if God cares about you, let me assure you that He does. If you've ever wondered if you have what it takes to make it in the Christian life, let me assure you that you do. You're exactly where God intends you to be, but you're not meant to stay in this place forever. God is on the move and He's working out His purposes in you and through you!

(Even in the midst of your trouble, doubt, and fear.) Before we dig into our Bible passage for the week, answer these self-examination questions:

How would you rate your faith in God right now on a scale of 1–10, with 1 being no faith and 10 being great faith?

What is a longing or dream you have that you have been waiting for God to fulfill? How hopeful have you remained of God's ability to fulfill this longing?

_____

_____

_____

Has God impressed on you a Bible passage in your season of waiting? When did you last get that sense of God speaking to you through His Word about your struggle?

_____

_____

_____

When we are waiting on God for something, it can cloud our spiritual sight. God has purpose for us in every task and person we interact with. When we are prayerfully aware, these times can become divine appointments in our day. Share a time you may have seen God working in the seemingly mundane spaces of your life.

_____

_____

The following passages from Genesis tell a bit of the story of Sarah, a woman with unshakable moxie.

Read Genesis 16:1–5; 18:1, 9–15; 21:1–7

Now Sarai, Abram's wife, had borne him no children. She had a female Egyptian servant whose name was Hagar. And Sarai said to Abram, "Behold now, the LORD has prevented me from bearing children. Go in to my servant; it may be that I shall obtain children by her." And Abram listened to the voice of Sarai. So, after Abram had lived ten years in the land of Canaan, Sarai, Abram's wife, took Hagar the Egyptian, her servant, and gave her to Abram her husband as a wife. And he went in to Hagar, and she conceived. And when she saw that she had conceived, she looked with contempt on her mistress. And Sarai said to Abram, "May the wrong done to me be on you! I gave my servant to your embrace, and when she saw that she had conceived, she looked on me with contempt. May the LORD judge between you and me!"

And the LORD appeared to him by the oaks of Mamre, as he sat at the door of his tent in the heat of the day.

[The three men] said to him, "Where is Sarah your wife?" And he said, "She is in the tent." The LORD said, "I will surely return to you about this time next year, and Sarah your wife shall have a son." And Sarah was listening at the tent door behind him. Now Abraham and Sarah were old, advanced in years. The way of women had ceased to be with Sarah. So Sarah laughed to herself, saying, "After I am worn out, and my lord is old, shall I have pleasure?" The LORD said to Abraham, "Why did Sarah laugh and say, 'Shall I indeed bear a child, now that I am old?' Is anything too hard for the LORD? At the appointed time I will return to you, about this time next year, and Sarah shall have a son." But Sarah denied it, saying, "I did not laugh," for she was afraid. He said, "No, but you did laugh."

The LORD visited Sarah as he had said, and the LORD did to Sarah as he had promised. And Sarah conceived and bore Abraham a son in his old age at the time of which God had spoken to him. Abraham called the name of his son who was born to him, whom Sarah bore him, Isaac. And Abraham circumcised his son Isaac when he was eight days old, as God had commanded him. Abraham was a hundred years old when his son Isaac was born to him. And Sarah said, "God has made laughter for me; everyone who hears will laugh over me." And she said, "Who would have said to Abraham that Sarah would nurse children? Yet I have borne him a son in his old age."

Questions to Ponder

Summarize the big idea of the story of Sarah. Is there anything in this story that surprises you about her?

_____

_____

_____

_____

In the first part of our reading, Sarah steps out and tries to create an opportunity for something to happen in her and Abraham's life. How did that turn out for her? Why?

_____

_____

_____

Why do you think God didn't stop Sarah and Abraham from taking matters into their own hands?

_____

_____

_____

The second section in our reading is even more fascinating. What is Sarah's response to God's promise to Abraham for a son with Sarah?

What can you learn about God from the way He responds to Sarah's laughter in Genesis 18?

_____

_____

_____

Sarah gave her husband another woman to have a child with in order to attempt to fulfill God's promise. Then she laughed and lied when God sent messengers to give a timeline for the promise. Does it surprise you that God would still keep His promise to Sarah and Abraham? Explain.

_____

_____

_____

Now let's jump to the last section in our reading. Describe the kind of laughter that Sarah expresses now. How is that different from the laughter earlier in the second section?

_____

_____

_____

In the third section, Sarah makes a statement that reveals her faith in God. How would you describe her faith at this point in time?

_____

_____

_____

As you consider God's fulfillment of His promise to Abraham and Sarah, how much of His purpose do you think hinged on the strength of Abraham and Sarah's faith?

_____

_____

_____

The longer I'm a Christian the more I am aware that God works not because of how much faith I have in Him, but despite my weak faith. It's always His faithfulness that tips the scale in my life for good. Sarah's story reminds us that it is God's goodness that makes all the difference in the world in our lives. In fact too often, just like Sarah, our response to God is either one of disbelief or of trying to take matters into our own hands.

Think of a time in your life when you tried to fix your own problems or tried to accomplish God's goals with your own strategies. What happened?

_____

_____

_____

_____

What is your go-to reaction when you struggle with faith? What is a circumstance that led you to that point? What eventually happened?

_____

_____

_____

_____

Even when we're tempted to fix our own problems, we can't. Even when we try to fulfill our own dreams, we fail. In time we start to learn that our inability to create our own destiny is the greatest grace of all because it becomes our very means to turn to God in need. And the moment we turn to Him is the moment we experience the freedom of knowing that there is something greater than what we think we need—and His name is Jesus!

Let's explore some verses on disappointment and see what God's Word tells us about His purposes for us when nothing seems to be happening in our lives.

Read Jeremiah 17:7–8. Describe what the year of drought might look like. What is God's promise to you in your year of drought?

_____

_____

_____

Read Philippians 1:6. What does this verse tell us about God's willingness and ability to carry us through to the fulfillment of His promises for us?

_____

_____

Read Jeremiah 29:11. How can this verse encourage you in seasons when you might feel the weight of disappointment?

_____

_____

Read Habakkuk 3:17–19. What are some of the things you can you count on even in the hardest seasons of your life?

_____

_____

Read James 1:2–4. Why does God allow trials in our lives?

_____

_____

Read James 1:12. What is the promise God gives to the one who perseveres?

_____

Read 1 Peter 1:6–7. What can we rejoice in in times of trials?

_____

_____

There are endless verses that talk about the human struggle to believe God. There are endless examples of men and women who wrestled with their faith and had to shift their expectations to line up with God's time-table and strategies. Yet over and over the theme is the same: God faithfully provides for His own and accomplishes His purposes for His people despite how wobbly their faith can be. The great story to be told is not of our faithfulness to God but of His faithfulness to us!

Have you ever struggled to believe God's faithfulness to you because of how faithless you've been? Read 2 Timothy 2:13. How does this verse encourage you right now?

_____

_____

There is one more aspect to the story of Sarah that we should spend a few minutes on. It's found in Hebrews 11:11–12.

> By faith Sarah herself received power to conceive, even when she was past the age, since she considered him faithful who had promised. Therefore from one man, and him as good as dead, were born descendants as many as the stars of heaven and as many as the innumerable grains of sand by the seashore.

What strikes you as the most incredible part of these verses?

_____

_____

As you consider what we read earlier about Sarah's attempt to have an heir through Hagar and her laughter about her own pregnancy, do you see a woman who was faithful in believing God's promises? Explain.

_____

_____

I'm fascinated by the reminder that God sees deeper than we do. He sees the very bottom of our hearts. I'm encouraged to understand not only God's faithfulness to us, but His willingness to see past our sometimes faithless actions to the depths of our hearts. Where we are prone to judge one another as weak in faith and become discouraged by our lives, God sees the thread of faith that is still hanging strong and refuses to let up. In Hebrews 11 we're given the reminder that Sarah, despite her struggle to believe, her need to manipulate, and her rush to see results, was in the depth of her heart a woman who loved God and longed for His promises. Sarah was a woman of unshakable moxie, resilient to her core.

Aren't you glad God doesn't judge us the way we judge one another? Aren't you glad that God sees past our actions and deep into our hearts? Journal your thoughts and thank God for seeing deep into your heart.

Application Questions

How is God equipping you to trust Him and receive His Grace? Choose one or more of the questions below to answer in the space provided.

- What are some ways you might change your expectations as you come to God in prayer?
- How does knowing what you know about God now help you to pray differently to Him or to worship Him more deeply?
- Spend time making a list of the ways God has been faithful in your life. How have you seen His love for you? Consider finding

an object to remind you of God's faithfulness in your life. Place this object in a prominent place so you are prompted to reflect on God's faithfulness regularly.

Lectio Divina

Our goal in this section is to experience the practice of quiet Scripture meditation in order to draw us closer to Jesus as a community. After each reading, answer the questions below, keeping your answers succinct and specific. Invite yourself to listen to God through His Word, allowing the Holy Spirit to move in you. Don't be afraid to share yourself authentically with others.

Habakkuk 3:17–19

Habakkuk Rejoices in the LORD

> Though the fig tree should not blossom,
>   nor fruit be on the vines,
> the produce of the olive fail
>   and the fields yield no food,
> the flock be cut off from the fold
>   and there be no herd in the stalls,
> yet I will rejoice in the LORD;
>   I will take joy in the God of my salvation.
> GOD, the Lord, is my strength;
>   he makes my feet like the deer's;
>   he makes me tread on my high places.

First Reading

What is one word or phrase that the Holy Spirit impresses on you?

_____

Second Reading

What do you feel? What specific situation in your life today relates to the passage?

_____

_____

_____

Third Reading

What is Christ's personal invitation to you from the Scripture?

_____

_____

Wrapping It Up

Consider sharing these quotes with your friends on social media.

> When we stop listening to all of the
> voices of the culture is when we start
> really hearing Him more clearly.
> —Lina AbuJamra

● ● ●

> In deconstructing, while so many things have
> changed, the core of who Jesus is and what
> He has done for us, His deep love for us, His
> unconditional commitment to us has been
> the fuel to help me rise up from the ashes.
> —Lina AbuJamra

● ● ●

> I refuse to accept defeat because there
> is a God who has overcome defeat.
> —Lina AbuJamra

● ● ●

> We stand undaunted. We stand unafraid.
> We stand unshaken by the things that
> normally shake us, not because of what
> we can do but because of what God has
> done in us through Christ Jesus.
> —Lina AbuJamra

● ● ●

Session 4

TRUSTING GOD IN THE DARK

Trust[6]
/'trəst/ noun

1 a: assured reliance on the character, ability, strength, or truth of someone or something
   b: one in which confidence is placed
2 a: dependence on something future or contingent : HOPE

This Week's Bible Study Goals

- Understand that the faithfulness of God is the truthfulness of His Word
- Learn to see the light of God's presence and comfort in your darkest places

Your Personal Goals for the Week

- Continue to share authentically and transparently with one another
- Continue to build trust within your group
- Ponder and talk about areas you wish to grow in
- Add any other goals you may have_____

_____

_____

_____

_____

Memory Verse

Before I was afflicted I went astray,
but now I keep your word.

Psalm 119:67

Get Started

When has God brought light into your dark moments?

_____

_____

_____

_____

How do you keep moving during the dark times in your life?

_____

_____

_____

_____

Briefly describe a time of suffering when God's Word comforted you. Share which passage(s) of Scripture helped you and how.

_____

_____

_____

_____

Meet Katie Lewis

While watching the video, record any observations, memorable moments, personal connections, or questions you have.

Video Discussion Questions

What stood out to you from the video?

How did you connect with the greenhouse illustration of dirt and flowers? Which season of life do you think you are in right now?

Has there ever been anything in your life that made you struggle to believe that God's Word is true? Explain.

When are God's promises the hardest for you to hang on to?

Bible Study

Complete this session during the week to discuss with your small group.

God's Word is true no matter what we're going through or what our feelings tell us! This is especially hard to believe when life is dark and God seems oblivious to our pain. When you stop and think about it, our culture today can seem to be tolerant of just about anything except for two things: that Jesus is the only path to salvation, and that the Bible is indeed the true Word of God. Yet for the follower of Jesus, nothing is more certain than the notion that God wrote a book, the Bible. He wrote it through thirty-five authors over a span of fifteen hundred years in sixty-six separate books that tell the same story: that Jesus is the only Savior for people who desperately need saving.

Throughout Scripture are reminders that the Bible is inspired by God through the Holy Spirit and that without this book we're lost. While the book itself is not magical, it is our means to know God and understand His ways. Yet despite being familiar with God's promises, too many Christians still struggle with believing them when life is hard. It's as if we don't know how to apply God's promises to our painful spaces. Perhaps we expected God to spare us our troubles, instead of understanding that it's His presence in our troubles that makes all the difference in the world. I've spent too much time being frustrated with God when His promises seemed too good to be true. Today I can look back and see God's hand guiding me and His truth lighting my way, especially when I was at my lowest.

I think one of our problems is that instead of making the Bible about God, we make it about ourselves. When we do this, we miss the point of God's Word, which is to awaken us to God and to deepen our understanding and our worship of Him. It took a while for me as a follower of Jesus to get into the habit of spending time with God through His Word. Even after years of habitually reading the Bible daily, it's easy to get into a rut of simply paging through the words of Scripture without a sense of God's nearness. Like Katie described in the video, I've been tempted to rush through my seasons of pain in hopes of getting to the more flowery parts of life. But it's in my seasons of pain that God's presence has been the nearest. I've had to learn to abide in God's Word when the answers to my problems are unclear.

Instead of approaching God's Word in a dutiful fashion, burdened by guilt and driven by striving for God's approval, my prayer is that you will encounter the Almighty in a more personal way as we explore God's Word together this week. Before you read this week's Bible passage, take some time to answer these questions:

As honestly as you can know it, what is your goal when you spend time in God's Word?

_____

_____

_____

What challenges do you encounter when trying to integrate meaningful time with God?

_____

_____

_____

Where in your life are you wrestling with God and His Word right now?

_____

_____

_____

Read Genesis 3:1–13

> Now the serpent was more crafty than any other beast of the field that the LORD God had made.
>
> He said to the woman, "Did God actually say, 'You shall not eat of any tree in the garden'?" And the woman said to the serpent, "We may eat of the fruit of the trees in the garden, but God said, 'You shall not eat of the fruit of the tree that is in the midst of the garden, neither shall you touch it, lest you die.'" But the serpent said to the woman, "You will not surely die. For God knows that when you eat of it your eyes will be opened, and you will be like God, knowing good and evil." So when the woman saw that the tree was good for food, and that it was a delight to the eyes, and that the tree was to be desired to make one wise, she took of its fruit and ate, and she also gave some to her husband who was with her, and he ate. Then the eyes of both were opened, and they knew that they were naked. And they sewed fig leaves together and made themselves loincloths.
>
> And they heard the sound of the LORD God walking in the garden in the cool of the day, and the man and his wife hid themselves from the presence of the LORD God among the trees of the garden. But the LORD God called to the man and said to him, "Where are you?" And he said, "I heard the sound of you in the garden, and I was afraid, because I was naked, and I hid myself." He said, "Who told you that you were naked? Have

you eaten of the tree of which I commanded you not to eat?" The man said, "The woman whom you gave to be with me, she gave me fruit of the tree, and I ate." Then the LORD God said to the woman, "What is this that you have done?" The woman said, "The serpent deceived me, and I ate."

Questions to Ponder

What do you think is at the heart of the battle that Eve goes through when she meets the serpent?

Why do you think Eve chose to listen to the serpent over the voice of God?

To better understand what was at the heart of Eve's temptation, you might want to read Genesis 2:16–17. What boundaries did God give Adam and Eve as it pertained to eating the fruit in the garden?

In what ways did the serpent twist God's words?

Why do you think Adam didn't recall God's instructions in the moment of temptation?

What was the outcome of Adam and Eve listening to the serpent's voice instead of God's? Why did Adam and Eve hide?

How did God respond to Adam and Eve after their fall?

The story of the fall, Adam and Eve's choice to sin, is foundational to our understanding of God's Word. After God created a perfect world with two perfect humans in it, it's hard to imagine that anything could have gone wrong! Adam and Eve had everything. They had a beautiful place to live. They had purpose in their lives. They had the unbroken fellowship with God. They had each other. Yet despite all that they had, all they could focus on was the one thing they did not have. And in their moment of weakness, they chose to ignore God's clear instruction, and the consequence of their decision continues to haunt us to this day.

It turns out that ignoring God's Word and trying to make up our own truth is deadly.

Today our culture continues to try the same strategy that's already been proven to fail. Each day we're given a choice: to believe God's Word and thrive, or to make up our own truth and suffer. It should be a no-brainer. Yet most of the world is consistently choosing anything except for submission to the truth of God's Word. Why is it so much more tempting to give in to a serpent in the garden than to the God who put us in the garden to begin with?

We have a choice when life is dark: to believe God's promises to be true, or to listen to the lies of the evil one. Let's take some time and dig into what God teaches us on the value of believing His Word when life is dark.

Read John 5:39. About whom does Scripture testify?

_____

_____

Read 2 Timothy 3:16. What do you learn about God's Word in this verse?

_____

_____

Read Romans 10:17. How does faith grow in our hearts?

_____

_____

Read James 1:2–5. What happens when our faith is tested through trials?

_____

_____

Read 2 Corinthians 1:8–10. What does Paul explain was one of the purposes of his dark trial? What hope did Paul hang on to in order to make it through the night?

_____

_____

Read Lamentations 3:22–33. This is one of my favorite passages of Scripture. I read it whenever I need to renew my hope. How might this passage or another passage help you renew your hope when you're at a low point?

_____

_____

_____

Read Psalm 119:105. Of what value is God's Word to the Christian?

_____

_____

Read Isaiah 40:8. Does God's Word change with the times and culture?

_____

_____

Read Psalm 27:13–14. What was the belief that kept the psalmist hopeful in waiting?

_____

_____

Read Philippians 4:8–9. How does this verse say we can have peace?

_____

_____

Read 1 Peter 5:7. Why should we cast our cares on the Lord?

_____

_____

_____

Read Joshua 21:45. How many of God's promises fail? How does this impact your hope in God?

_____

_____

_____

While I realize that that was a lot of verses to take in, the point should be obvious: we need God's Word to sustain us when we're trudging through the dirt!

When we internalize the harsh reality of Adam and Eve's choice to sin in the garden, we can avoid living in shame if we choose God's Word over what feels good in the moment.

Think of a time when you did what you wanted to do instead of what you know God was asking you to do. What consequences did you suffer?

_____

_____

Let's read Genesis 3:20–24.

The truth is that we will inevitably fail. We will choose our immediate comfort over God's promises. We want immediate gratification rather than the pleasure of God. It's why we need Jesus! But Genesis 3:20–24 gives us hope.

What was God's reaction to Adam and Eve's sin?

_____

_____

How did God provide for them after their fall? What was the significance of the garment of skin that God made Adam and Eve?

_____

_____

Why do you think God put Adam and Eve out of the Garden of Eden? In what ways was that an act of grace?

_____

_____

God—who created everything and could end it all in a blink of an eye—reveals His extravagant grace so deeply that we're left dumbfounded by it! It's in Genesis 3:15 that the first mention of the coming of Jesus is alluded to. He is the promised "offspring" who would crush the power of sin and the devil. The rest of the biblical narrative is spent on pointing to this Messiah who would one day come to pay the price for the sins of Adam and Eve, and for our sins! Aren't you glad that our God is a God of mercy and grace? Even in the darkest chapter of humanity, God's light shines with the promise of Jesus!

As we wrap up this week together, let's bring back our attention to what it means to be a woman of moxie. One of the best ways to show strength and courage, especially when we're walking through dark times, is to choose to follow the truth of God's Word over the things our broken world promises but cannot fully deliver. A woman of strength refuses to give in to the lies of Satan when God's Word is sure and secure. A woman of moxie understands that to sacrifice personal comfort for holiness is no sacrifice at all if it brings us a little closer to the heart of our Father. A woman of moxie learns to see God's goodness even in our darkest places and trusts the outcome of our trials to God's goodness. A woman of moxie banks everything on the grace of God whose love is clearly seen in the pages of His Word and in the face of His Son, Jesus. A woman of moxie goes with God despite what she sees or doesn't see right now. Are you a woman of moxie? How does your life reflect this moxie? How do you want your life to show moxie?

Application Questions

How is God equipping you to trust Him and receive His grace? Choose one or more of the questions below to answer in the space provided.

- As you consider the story of Eve, think about yourself. Are you easily persuaded by the lies of the serpent or are you hanging on boldly to the truth of God's Word? Explain.

- The more our culture deviates from God's Word, the harder it will be to hold on to what God's Word teaches. How much are you willing to sacrifice in order to continue to live according to God's Word? How will you give God your time? Your attention? Your trust?

- Consider a challenge you are facing. Find one or two Bible verses related to your situation. Put the Scripture "to the test," as Katie mentioned in the video. Ask God to help you to put these verses in action. Wait expectantly as you seek the validity of the Scriptures.

- If you could create a piece of jewelry or other art to symbolize your journey with God, what would it be? Consider making something to remind you of your journey.

Lectio Divina

Our goal in this section is to experience the practice of quiet Scripture meditation in order to draw us closer to Jesus as a community. After each reading, answer the questions below, keeping your answers succinct and specific. Invite yourself to listen to God through His Word, allowing the Holy Spirit to move in you. Don't be afraid to share yourself authentically with others.

Isaiah 40:27–31

> Why do you say, O Jacob,
>   and speak, O Israel,
> "My way is hidden from the LORD,
>   and my right is disregarded by my God"?
> Have you not known? Have you not heard?
> The LORD is the everlasting God,
>   the Creator of the ends of the earth.
> He does not faint or grow weary;
>   his understanding is unsearchable.
> He gives power to the faint,
>   and to him who has no might he increases strength.
> Even youths shall faint and be weary,
>   and young men shall fall exhausted;
> but they who wait for the LORD shall renew their
>   strength;
>   they shall mount up with wings like eagles;
> they shall run and not be weary;
>   they shall walk and not faint.

First Reading

What is one word or phrase that the Holy Spirit impresses on you?

_____

Second Reading

What do you feel? What specific situation in your life today relates to the passage?

_____

_____

Third Reading

What is Christ's personal invitation to you from the Scripture?

Wrapping It Up

Consider sharing these quotes with your friends on social media.

> Without dirt, you don't have flowers.
> —Katie Lewis

● ● ●

> God redeems every bit of our brokenness.
> He's our light in the darkness.
> —Lina AbuJamra

● ● ●

> We have a choice when life is dark: to
> believe God's promises to be true, or
> to listen to the lies of the evil one.
> —Lina AbuJamra

● ● ●

LEANING ON THE HOLY SPIRIT'S POWER

Power[7]

pow·er /ˈpaů(-ə)r/ noun

1 a: ability to act or produce an effect
2 a: possession of control, authority, or influence over others

transitive verb

1 : to supply with power and especially motive power
2 : to give impetus to

This Week's Bible Study Goals

- Understand the power of the Holy Spirit in your life
- Resolve to yield to the power of the Holy Spirit in your life

Your Personal Goals for the Week

- Admit your willingness to go where the Spirit of God wants you to go and to do what He wants you to do
- Continue to share authentically and transparently with one another
- Ponder and talk about areas you wish to grow in
- Add any other goals you may have_____

_____

_____

Memory Verse

But you will receive power when the Holy Spirit comes upon you; and you will be my witnesses in Jerusalem and in all Judea and Samaria, and to the ends of the earth.

Acts 1:8

Get Started

Share about a time when you struggled to let go of anger toward someone.

_____

_____

_____

_____

What comes to your mind when you think about the Holy Spirit? What questions do you have about the Holy Spirit?

_____

_____

_____

_____

Share about a time in your life when you were keenly aware of the power of the Holy Spirit.

_____

_____

_____

_____

Why do you think so many Christians live oblivious to the life-changing power of the Holy Spirit?

Meet Bernice King

While watching the video, record any observations, memorable moments, personal connections, or questions you have.

Video Discussion Questions

What stood out to you from the video?

_____

_____

Bernice talked about the Holy Spirit as a person. Did that change the way you perceive the Spirit's place in your life? Explain.

_____

_____

Have you ever experienced human comfort through a hug? Journal your thoughts on Bernice's connection between one hug and the comfort of the Holy Spirit.

_____

_____

_____

In what ways did Bernice's demeanor reflect the power of the Spirit in her life?

_____

_____

Where in your life do you long for more of the Spirit? How did Bernice's story inspire you to want to yield to the Spirit even more deeply?

_____

_____

_____

Bible Study

Complete this session during the week to discuss with your small group.

Some people are easier to forgive than others. Like the guy who cut me off in traffic the other day. While his arrogance made me mad, I was able to let it go after a couple of stop lights. Or the barista who didn't put enough cream in my coffee. She was forgiven by the time lunch came around.

Then there are some real doozies I've had to wrestle with. Like the word spoken harshly to me ten Christmases ago by that one relative. Or the pastor who betrayed our church with his poor choices and left the entire congregation picking up the broken pieces of our faith.

I've struggled with my share of anger and bitterness toward people who have hurt me. One of my favorite stories about forgiveness is from the life of Corrie ten Boom. Cornelia "Corrie" ten Boom (April 15, 1892–April 15, 1983) was a Dutch Christian watchmaker who helped many Jews escape the Nazi Holocaust during World War II. She was imprisoned for her actions and eventually wrote her story in her famous biography, *The Hiding Place*. You could say she had a lot of baggage in her life when it came to forgiveness. She once told a story to express exactly how hard it was for her to learn to forgive as Christ forgives us.

In the story, Corrie recalls that she had just finished speaking about forgiveness at a church meeting when she saw a heavyset man in the congregation making his way toward her. She instantly recognized the man. He had been a guard in the concentration camp where Corrie and her now dead sister Betsie were imprisoned. She had been mocked and shamed and forced to walk naked past this very man.

Some people are harder to forgive than others. Here was Corrie ten Boom, supposedly the expert on forgiveness, put to the test face-to-face with her greatest enemy. The soldier went on to tell Corrie that he had become a Christian. As he stretched out his hand to shake hers, he said: "I know that God has forgiven me for the cruel things I did there, but I would like to hear it from your lips as well. Fräulein, will you forgive me?"

Corrie ten Boom had a decision to make. Would she, could she, do the unthinkable? Corrie knew all about the message of forgiveness. She understood it as a command of God. She had received Christ's forgiveness for her. But could she now do the one thing she could not imagine doing?

"If you do not forgive men their trespasses," Jesus says, "neither will your Father in heaven forgive your trespasses." As she thought about Christ's words, Corrie ten Boom writes that she thrust out her hand to the one stretched out to her, and then experienced an incredible thing: "The current started in my shoulder, raced down my arm, sprang into our joined hands. And then this healing warmth seemed to flood my whole being, bringing tears to my eyes."

"I forgive you, brother!" I cried. "With all my heart!"[8]

The two grasped each other's hands, the former guard and the former prisoner. Corrie wrote that she had never known God's love so intensely as she did then.

Corrie's story is not so different from the story of Bernice King. Like Corrie, the challenge was to forgive what felt unforgiveable. For Bernice, like Corrie, there was healing power in human touch. For Bernice, like Corrie, the truth about God's love had to translate into the liberating experience of God's love.

Most of us struggle with the same thing. We long to change in the most challenging areas of our lives but lack the power to do so. Where *does* a Christian get the power to change?

For both Bernice King and Corrie ten Boom, it seems like there was a divine power that propelled them to do the unthinkable. That power is the power of the Holy Spirit, so clearly explained by Bernice, and His power is available to every man or woman who accepts Jesus as Savior. Sadly, most Christians never grasp exactly how powerful we could be if only we yielded to the power of the Holy Spirit in our lives. Most Christians live oblivious to the very presence of the Holy Spirit in us. Our tendency is to think of the power of the Spirit as something we can use, as opposed to a person we can rely on and live with.

This week we're going to tap into this power, the power of the Holy Spirit. As we start this week's journey together, if you have been wrestling to let go of pain and anger, won't you ask the Spirit of God to give you what you need to let go of the pain and anger that you've been carrying? Are you willing to let God guide you down this path toward change and freedom?

In what one specific area in your Christian life have you struggled to change?

Describe some of the frustration and emotion you've felt in the times you've tried to live the Christian life without the help of the Holy Spirit.

_____

_____

If your life was filmed with a hidden camera, what story would your demeanor and daily emotional state tell about your faith in God?

_____

_____

On a scale of 1–10 how yielded would you say you are to the Holy Spirit in your life?

Not yielded   Fully yielded

1   2   3   4   5   6   7   8   9   10

Read John 14:15–29

> "If you love me, you will keep my commandments. And I will ask the Father, and he will give you another Helper, to be with you forever, even the Spirit of truth, whom the world cannot receive, because it neither sees him nor knows him. You know him, for he dwells with you and will be in you.
>
> "I will not leave you as orphans; I will come to you. Yet a little while and the world will see me no more, but you will see me. Because I live, you also will live. In that day you will know that I am in my Father, and you in me, and I in you. Whoever has my commandments and keeps them, he it is who loves me. And he who loves me will be loved by my Father, and I will love him and manifest myself to him." Judas (not Iscariot) said to him, "Lord, how is it that you will manifest yourself to us, and not to the world?" Jesus answered him, "If anyone loves me, he will keep my word, and my Father will love him, and we will come to him and make our home with him. Whoever does not love me does not keep my words. And the word that you hear is not mine but the Father's who sent me.

"These things I have spoken to you while I am still with you. But the Helper, the Holy Spirit, whom the Father will send in my name, he will teach you all things and bring to your remembrance all that I have said to you. Peace I leave with you; my peace I give to you. Not as the world gives do I give to you. Let not your hearts be troubled, neither let them be afraid. You heard me say to you, 'I am going away, and I will come to you.' If you loved me, you would have rejoiced, because I am going to the Father, for the Father is greater than I. And now I have told you before it takes place, so that when it does take place you may believe."

Questions to Ponder

What is your first reaction to these words that Jesus spoke?

As you read the passage, what are some of the ways you would describe the Holy Spirit? What are some specific functions of the Holy Spirit that Jesus outlines in this passage?

Picture yourself sitting with Jesus and listening to Him speak these words to you. What emotions do you experience as you receive His promise of the Holy Spirit?

How does Jesus describe the relationship between the Holy Spirit and His followers? Is it an intellectual relationship or an intimate one? How intimate is your relationship with the Holy Spirit? What stands in the way of your awareness of His presence in your life?

_____

_____

_____

Jesus knew that the only way we would make it in this life is through the power of the Holy Spirit. In the days leading up to His death, Jesus spent a whole lot of time talking to His disciples about the Holy Spirit and His role in their lives. Later on, the apostle Paul built on our understanding of the role of the Holy Spirit in our lives.

The following verses are meant to help us learn more about the Holy Spirit and the place He longs to have in our lives.

Read Genesis 1:1–2. It's easy to think about the Holy Spirit as someone who started His work in the New Testament. What does the account of creation tell you about the Holy Spirit's existence?

_____

_____

Read Ephesians 1:13–14. What does the apostle Paul teach about when we receive the Holy Spirit?

_____

_____

Read 1 Corinthians 12:13. In your own words, describe how the Holy Spirit unifies Christians. How does that change the way you view the brother or sister in Christ that you might not like as much as the others?

_____

_____

Let's look at some of the roles of the Holy Spirit in our lives. For each verse, write down what the Holy Spirit promises you:

John 14:26

_____

_____

John 15:26

_____

_____

John 16:7–8

_____

_____

Romans 8:26–27

_____

_____

1 Corinthians 12:4–11

_____

_____

2 Corinthians 3:16–18

_____

_____

Read 1 Corinthians 2:10–16. What does God's Word teach about the difference between followers of Jesus and the rest of the world as it pertains to the Holy Spirit's presence and work?

_____

_____

Read 1 Corinthians 6:19. How much ownership does the Holy Spirit want in your life? When you think about who the person of the Spirit is, why does it sound more reasonable for Him to demand so much?

_____

_____

Read Ephesians 4:30. Paul writes that the Holy Spirit can be grieved. In what ways can we grieve the Holy Spirit?

_____

_____

Read Psalm 139:7–10. When we think about grieving the Holy Spirit, it's easy to feel discouragement and distance from God. What do the words of King David remind you about God's faithfulness to you?

_____

_____

Read Galatians 5:22–23. Which of the fruit of the Spirit do you feel you need the most in your life right now? How might God be using the circumstances and people in your life to produce more of that fruit?

_____

_____

Read Acts 1:8. Jesus promised the disciples Holy Spirit power. What did the power of the Holy Spirit look like for the disciples in the early church?

Read Romans 15:13. This is my favorite verse on the power of the Holy Spirit. What emotions fill you as you read the words of Paul here?

Application Questions

How is God equipping you to trust Him and receive His grace? Choose one or more of the questions below to answer in the space provided.

- In light of all we've learned about the Holy Spirit, how does knowing you have God's power in you through the Holy Spirit encourage you to change in the areas in your life where you're experiencing defeat?
- Are you fully yielded to the Holy Spirit in your life or is there anything you're still holding back from God?
- Are you willing to let go of whatever it is that you've been unwilling to surrender to God? Some of the most common things I've struggled to let go of are relationships I long for, dreams I pine for, addictions I can't imagine living without, and sometimes harmless things that become my places of comfort. What might you be struggling to let go of right now? Spend time in prayer giving these things to God, ask the Holy Spirit to help you let go of anything you are holding too tightly to.
- Is there someone you need to confess to or come clean about a wrong that has been weighing you down? Perhaps you've been wronged and have been holding on to a grudge. Explore how releasing that grudge can make you feel freer or lighter. Sometimes forgiveness is humanly impossible. But the Holy Spirit is able to help. If you are struggling, ask the Spirit for His help.

Lectio Divina

Our goal in this section is to experience the practice of quiet Scripture meditation in order to draw us closer to Jesus as a community. After each reading, answer the questions below, keeping your answers succinct and specific. Invite yourself to listen to God through His Word, allowing the Holy Spirit to move in you. Don't be afraid to share yourself authentically with others.

Acts 3:1–10

> Now Peter and John were going up to the temple at the hour of prayer, the ninth hour. And a man lame from birth was being carried, whom they laid daily at the gate of the temple that is called the Beautiful Gate to ask alms of those entering the temple. Seeing Peter and John about to go into the temple, he asked to receive alms. And Peter directed his gaze at him, as did John, and said, "Look at us." And he fixed his attention on them, expecting to receive something from them. But Peter said, "I have no silver and gold, but what I do have I give to you. In the name of Jesus Christ of Nazareth, rise up and walk!" And he took him by the right hand and raised him up, and immediately his feet and ankles were made strong. And leaping up, he stood and began to walk, and entered the temple with them, walking and leaping and praising God. And all the people saw him walking and praising God, and recognized him as the one who sat at the Beautiful Gate of the temple, asking for alms. And they were filled with wonder and amazement at what had happened to him.

First Reading

What is one word or phrase that the Holy Spirit impresses on you?

Second Reading

What do you feel? What specific situation in your life today relates to the passage?

Third Reading

What is Christ's personal invitation to you from the Scripture?

Wrapping It Up

Consider sharing these quotes with your friends on social media.

> *Many Christians live oblivious to the life-changing power of the Holy Spirit.*
>
> —Lina AbuJamra

● ● ●

> *Our tendency is to think of the power of the Spirit as something we can use, as opposed to a person we can rely on and live with.*
>
> —Lina AbuJamra

● ● ●

> *Most Christians never grasp exactly how powerful we could be if only we yielded to the power of the Holy Spirit in our lives.*
>
> —Lina AbuJamra

● ● ●

Session 6

PERSEVERING WITH HOPE

Hope[9]
/'hōp/ verb

intransitive verb

1: to cherish a desire with anticipation: to want something to happen or be true
   hopes for a promotion, *hoping* for the best, I *hope* so.
2: archaic : TRUST

transitive verb

1: to desire with expectation of obtainment or fulfillment
   I *hope* she remembers. *hopes* to be invited
2: to expect with confidence : TRUST
   Your mother is doing well, I *hope*.

This Week's Bible Study Goals

- Understand that Jesus alone is all the hope that you need
- Resolve to persevere in hope in the most painful seasons in your life

Your Personal Goals for the Week

- Continue to share as truthfully as possible with your group all that the Holy Spirit is teaching you
- Ponder and talk about all the ways you have seen God transform you into a woman of moxie
- Build confidence in God's promises as you go through suffering
- Add any other goals you may have_____

_____

Memory Verse

*May the God of hope fill you with all joy and
peace in believing, so that by the power of the
Holy Spirit you may abound in hope.*

Romans 15:13

Get Started

Share about a time in your life where you wanted to quit or give up on life
or on a particular situation.

_____

_____

_____

_____

Who is your greatest inspiration in the seasons in your life when you feel
like quitting?

_____

_____

_____

_____

What are some of the reasons you want to quit?

_____

_____

_____

_____

Meet Joni Eareckson Tada

While watching the video, record any observations, memorable moments, personal connections, or questions you have.

Video Discussion Questions

What stood out to you from the video?

_____

_____

_____

What was the turning point for Joni to finally find hope again in the midst of her pain?

_____

_____

Can you relate with Joni's love for Scripture and singing, and how singing praise to God or quoting Scripture in her pain has often helped her get stronger?

_____

_____

What are some ways you've learned to focus on God in order to deal with your pain or life challenges?

_____

_____

How did the video challenge you to think about perseverance and hope in your own life?

_____

_____

Bible Study

Complete this session during the week to discuss with your small group.

The first time I quit anything I was in my mid-twenties. It was during my Pediatric Emergency Medicine fellowship in Florida. For two years I waited for Starbucks to open a store near my house. I dreamed about it until one day the store opened and I signed up to work there. You could argue that it wasn't my best idea, but I was too pumped up about the new coffee shop to care. I was two months into my stint as a barista, saving kids' lives by day and making cappuccinos by night, when I woke up one Saturday morning too worn out to go to work. I thought I could call in. I dialed the manager and explained that I had had a really rough week and would not be showing up that evening. She freaked out a little and insisted I show up. It took me a moment to respond, and what came out of my mouth surprises me to this day. "I quit." And that was the end of that chapter.

When I showed up to the ER the next week and told everyone that I had quit my job at Starbucks, I discovered that the folks in the ER had a pool going on how long I would last. I also learned a very important lesson that day: sometimes the very places we long for become the places we can't wait to escape.

We all long to escape something. It might be a painful marriage, or a painful job, or it might be a painful health crisis, or a painful ministry or church environment. We try to fake it until we can make it, but eventually, we become too worn out to care. We start going through the motions.

We lose hope.

Hopelessness is one of the direst pitfalls for the follower of Jesus. A lifetime of Bible verses memorized become forgotten. A list of saints who have gone before us fade in our rear-view mirror. We become so focused on our pain that we lose sight of everything and everyone except the need to find relief. We become certain that escaping our situation will provide that relief.

Many turn to vice in order to numb the pain of their hopelessness. Some choose apathy as a more respectable alternative to quitting. We show up to our life but we're not really there. We start to feel unseen, unknown, unloved, which only feeds the loop of hopelessness even more.

If you've ever felt like quitting, you know exactly what I'm talking about. Your life hasn't turned out quite like you wanted it to. Maybe you're in that place right now. You're flirting with quitting. You don't see a way out. This week we're going for hope. We're going to dig into God's Word and ask His Spirit to restore us back to life.

I know He can do it because I've been to the pitfall of hopelessness more times than I care to admit, and I've survived. I'm still here. I'm still breathing. Some would argue that I'm thriving, but the jury's still out on that. I hope our time together will ignite your heart again with love for Jesus. The only way it will happen is if you're willing to reach out just a little bit even to touch the hem of His robe with faith like the woman we will read about. But before we dig into our Scripture for this week, let's take a moment and answer these questions.

Is there an area in your life where you have already given up hope or are about to?

_____

_____

If you could tell Jesus anything about your pain, what would you say? Try writing it out.

_____

_____

Why do you think hope is such a big deal to the follower of Jesus?

_____

_____

Read Mark 5:21–34

> And when Jesus had crossed again in the boat to the other side, a great crowd gathered about him, and he was beside the sea. Then came one of the rulers of the synagogue, Jairus by name, and seeing him, he fell at his feet and implored him earnestly, saying, "My little daughter is at the point of death. Come and lay your hands on her, so that she may be made well and live." And he went with him.

And a great crowd followed him and thronged about him. And there was a woman who had had a discharge of blood for twelve years, and who had suffered much under many physicians, and had spent all that she had, and was no better but rather grew worse. She had heard the reports about Jesus and came up behind him in the crowd and touched his garment. For she said, "If I touch even his garments, I will be made well." And immediately the flow of blood dried up, and she felt in her body that she was healed of her disease. And Jesus, perceiving in himself that power had gone out from him, immediately turned about in the crowd and said, "Who touched my garments?" And his disciples said to him, "You see the crowd pressing around you, and yet you say, 'Who touched me?'" And he looked around to see who had done it. But the woman, knowing what had happened to her, came in fear and trembling and fell down before him and told him the whole truth. And he said to her, "Daughter, your faith has made you well; go in peace, and be healed of your disease."

Questions to Ponder

What was the main problem that the woman in the story had?

What do you think drew her to Jesus?

What were some of the risks that the woman took when she showed up for healing?

Why do you think Jesus called her out instead of just letting her enjoy her healing?

_____

_____

Does it surprise you that no one else had noticed the woman until Jesus pointed her out? Explain.

_____

_____

How did Jesus respond to the woman's fear? What do you think of Jesus's response?

_____

_____

_____

When you consider Mark 5, the story of the woman with the issue of blood almost seems like an interruption between the crowd gathering around Jesus, the request for Jesus to go heal Jairus's daughter, and the actual healing of Jairus's daughter. I don't think the placement of the story is accidental. I've wondered if perhaps God meant to reinforce to us the notion that every interruption is divine. Even more personally speaking, I believe too many of us feel like our problems are a bother to Jesus. We live our lives on the outside looking in, hoping for hope, but expecting nothing but empty promises. We live our lives wishing to be healed, afraid to be seen, on the verge of giving up with just enough energy to quietly sit in the shadows of the last row of whatever space we're in. We desire to be seen but still cower in fear. We reach out to Jesus with no expectation that He'll ever notice us and are flabbergasted when He—without hesitation—stops and calls us His own.

Have you ever felt like an interruption to the flow of the Christian community?

Have you ever been ashamed of letting other people see your deepest pain?

How does the story of the woman give you strength to persevere in reaching out to Jesus?

Hope. It's what propels us to move toward Jesus. It's at the root of all we believe. I'm not talking about wishful thinking but about our own confidence, albeit weak at times, that Jesus will do what He is known to do. Jesus will fulfill His promises to us. Jesus will be all we expect Him to be. Too many of us are afraid to reach out to Him. Yet it's when we do reach out that we're given the power to persevere.

Let's meditate on a few Bible verses about hope as we move our hearts toward Jesus.

Read Ephesians 1:15–23. What is Paul's prayer for believers here? What is that hope that he refers to?

Read 1 Peter 1:3–5. What is the hope that Peter talks about here?

Read Colossians 1:27. Who is the hope of glory? What does this mean to you?

Read Hebrews 11:1. What is the connection between faith and hope?

Read Hebrews 10:23. Why can we hold on to hope? How does remembering God's faithfulness help?

Read Psalm 33:18. What is the promise for those who hope in God's unfailing love? What does living with this kind of hope look like for you?

Read Psalm 130:5. Where can we tangibly place our hope? How does knowing God's Word help give us hope?

Read Romans 5:2–5. What is the connection between suffering and hope?

Read Romans 15:13. Whose job is it to fill you with hope? What can we do to position ourselves in that hope?

Read Hebrews 6:17–20. What is the anchor that the writer of Hebrews refers to in these verses?

Everything about the Christian faith is linked to hope: hope that what God—who does not lie—has promised will come true; hope that centers on the person of Jesus Christ; hope that looks past our present trials and keeps on keeping on, not because of how strong we are but because of all Christ is. The power of Christ in us is the power the Christian holds over pain and tragedy and hopelessness. It's the power of the resurrection and it's the power that sets us free! While many of us look for earthly healing and miracles to rest our hope in, we have been given a far greater hope, one that does not ever waver, and it is the reality of the resurrected Christ now living in us.

Do you know this hope? Do you own it like a boss? Perhaps like the woman with the issue of blood, you have just enough faith to reach out and touch the hem of Christ's robe? The good news today is that even a little bit of faith in a big God of hope is enough (see Matthew 17:20)!

So go ahead, reach out to the hem of His robe and find healing. He is trustworthy.

Application Questions

How is God equipping you to trust Him and receive His grace? Choose one or more of the questions below to answer in the space provided.

- What does reaching out to touch the hem of Christ's robe look like to you right now?
- Has there ever been a time in your life where you saw that the greatest miracle you will ever be given is not the gift of healing but the gift of Christ's presence with you always? Have you observed this in anyone else? Explain what you observed.
- What are some promises from God's Word that you can rest your hope in in your areas of pain? Create something tangible to help you remember these promises.
- What are some ways others can pray for you when it comes to persevering in hope?

- What are some songs you can sing and Scriptures you can meditate on to help you cling to Jesus especially when you are in pain?

Lectio Divina

Our goal in this section is to experience the practice of quiet Scripture meditation in order to draw us closer to Jesus as a community. After each reading, answer the questions below, keeping your answers succinct and specific. Invite yourself to listen to God through His Word, allowing the Holy Spirit to move in you. Don't be afraid to share yourself authentically with others.

Psalm 42

As a deer pants for flowing streams,
    so pants my soul for you, O God.
My soul thirsts for God,
    for the living God.
When shall I come and appear before God?
My tears have been my food
    day and night,
while they say to me all the day long,
    "Where is your God?"
These things I remember,
    as I pour out my soul:
how I would go with the throng
    and lead them in procession to the house of God
with glad shouts and songs of praise,
    a multitude keeping festival.

Why are you cast down, O my soul,
    and why are you in turmoil within me?
Hope in God; for I shall again praise him,
    my salvation and my God.

My soul is cast down within me;
    therefore I remember you
from the land of Jordan and of Hermon,
    from Mount Mizar.
Deep calls to deep
    at the roar of your waterfalls;
all your breakers and your waves
    have gone over me.
By day the LORD commands his steadfast love,
    and at night his song is with me,
    a prayer to the God of my life.

I say to God, my rock:
    "Why have you forgotten me?
Why do I go mourning
    because of the oppression of the enemy?"
As with a deadly wound in my bones,
    my adversaries taunt me,
while they say to me all the day long,
    "Where is your God?"

Why are you cast down, O my soul,
    and why are you in turmoil within me?
Hope in God; for I shall again praise him,
    my salvation and my God.

First Reading

What is one word or phrase that the Holy Spirit impresses on you?

Second Reading

What do you feel? What specific situation in your life today relates to the passage?

Third Reading

What is Christ's personal invitation to you from the Scripture?

Wrapping It Up

Consider sharing these quotes with your friends on social media.

*Suffering is a textbook that will
teach you who you are.*
—Joni Eareckson Tada

● ● ●

*Suffering is a frightening friend but it's
a friend nonetheless. It ushers us into
relationship with Christ and His suffering.*
—Joni Eareckson Tada

● ● ●

*When we are at our worst points of
weakness and humbled before others,
mysterious, wonderful things can happen.*
—Joni Eareckson Tada

● ● ●

FINAL WORDS
FROM LINA

I hope you've enjoyed the last six weeks together. It's been a privilege to walk you through this Bible study to better frame what it looks like to be a woman of moxie from a biblical perspective.

As you've watched the six stories of amazing women of moxie (including yours truly), I hope you've been able to see that the kind of strength that God calls us to is not always what we assume it should be. Most of us living in today's culture have grown up with the world's view of what a strong woman should look like. We picture someone who is independent and assertive, can go toe to toe with anyone, and can run the world from the living room or the board room. We're encouraged as women to fight for our rights and to raise our voices and claim our places, and we're lauded when we refuse to stand down—for anyone. We are pressed not to admit any weakness—ever.

We've looked deeper at God's Word and hopefully now better understand God's perspective on what true strength and biblical moxie is. God's view challenges our culture deeply. Society today doesn't value a biblical worldview. God's view of strength is best seen in meekness and dependence. He sees who we really are in Christ and lovingly reminds us that we are His beloved children. He understands our struggles in trial and considers it His honor to give us His strength in our weaknesses and failures. God's perspective on strength is full of grace to those who feel they can't make it one more day. His eyes "run to and fro throughout the whole earth, to give strong support to those whose heart is blameless toward him" (2 Chronicles 16:9), not to those who try to prove they are worthy of Him.

None of us are worthy of God's favor. We are simply lavished by His love because of Jesus. When you think about it, it's Jesus who is at the heart of everything we call moxie. Because of Jesus, we're given a new identity.

Because of Jesus, we have the strength to overcome any trial. Because of Jesus, we can let go of our self-centered expectations. Because of Jesus, we can experience complete and undeserved forgiveness and in turn offer this same love and forgiveness to others.

If you want to know how much moxie you have, one way to find out is to stop and think about how much Jesus is filling your life today. The amount of power you experience to live a victorious, triumphant Christian life is directly proportional to the freedom you give the Holy Spirit to be the Lord of your life.

No matter where you started this journey toward moxie, I hope that you not only agree with Isaiah the prophet but are also taking intentional steps to live the words he wrote in Isaiah 30:15: "In returning and rest you shall be saved; in quietness and in trust shall be your strength."

Now *that's* moxie—rest, quietness, dependence, trust.

The question I leave you with is this: Are you willing to follow the Jesus way toward moxie?

I hope your answer is yes.

I hope that all you want is more of Jesus all the time.

NOTES

1. *Merriam-Webster*, s.v. "moxie," accessed September 11, 2023, https://www.merriam-webster.com/dictionary/moxie.
2. *Merriam-Webster's Collegiate Dictionary*, 11th ed. (2003), s.v. "grace."
3. Dallas Willard, *Renewing the Christian Mind: Essays, Interviews, and Talks*, ed. Gary Black Jr. (New York: HarperOne, 2016), 12.
4. C. S. Lewis, *The Problem of Pain* (San Francisco: HarperSanFrancisco, 2001), 91.
5. *Merriam-Webster*, s.v. "resilient," accessed September 11, 2023, https://merriam-webster.com/dictionary/resilient.
6. *Merriam-Webster*, s.v. "trust," accessed September 11, 2023, https://www.merriam-webster.com/dictionary/trust.
7. *Merriam-Webster*, s.v. "power," accessed September 11, 2023, https://www.merriam-webster.com/dictionary/power.
8. Corrie ten Boom, with Jamie Buckingham, *Tramp for the Lord* (London: Hodder & Stoughton, 1975), 218.
9. *Merriam-Webster*, s.v. "hope," accessed September 11, 2023, https://www.merriam-webster.com/dictionary/hope.

Spread the Word
by Doing One Thing.

- Give a copy of this book as a gift.

- Share the QR code link via your social media.

- Write a review of this book on your blog, favorite bookseller's website, or at ODB.org/store.

- Recommend this book to your church, small group, or book club.

Connect with us. [f] [o] [y]

Our Daily Bread Publishing
PO Box 3566, Grand Rapids, MI 49501, USA
Email: books@odb.org

Love God. Love Others.

with  Our Daily Bread.

Your gift changes lives.

Connect with us. [f] [◎] 🐦

Our Daily Bread Publishing
PO Box 3566, Grand Rapids, MI 49501, USA
Email: books@odb.org